Natural Causes

Pitt Poetry Series

Ed Ochester, Editor

Natural Causes

Mark Cox

To Lee & Nancy,
Hope this pleases you.
Love,

University of Pittsburgh Press

The publication of this book is supported by a grant

from the Pennsylvania Council on the Arts

Published by the University of Pittsburgh Press, Pittsburgh, Pa., 15260

ISBN 0-8229-5839-2

For Karin—*heart of my heart*

Contents

ONE

Ashes, Ashes

Adulthood's frost heaves tamped down,
that blank page smoothed,

a last glance up,
palm on the burnished rail.

That night, so many nights ago,
that house still as this one is now,

and you, sleepless below the attic dormer,
your face cold, quilts heavy as soil,

all the wind-burnt children, hearts quieted,
your snow tunnels welling with moonlight,

the farmyard evanescent
with mist and thickening ice.

How many splitting, warping, hand-hewn steps
between there and here, no elders

left at Scrabble around the kitchen table?
Unpoured and prepared again to be,

is this too much to ask?
To come to that young body

as to the mouth of a cave,
to reenter it and find

one's final shape in the accruing snow?

The land is only ground now.
No footpaths, no ruins, not even
a slab where the root cellar stood.
Still, there is the slap of a screen door
when my son exits the car,
the squeal of a well pump
when my youngest wants juice,
and there I am in the sprouting field corn,
back brown as mud, crew cut blond
as the pail of eggs I've never put down.

The adults are still patient,
awaiting breakfast in their graves,
the bacon still diminishing
in the blackened pan.
No one knows where I am.
Half-grown, tousled candle of a boy,
I have walked to where the vulture landed,
to his runway of symmetrical rows
where the fox, lame with poison,
swallowed her last breath.
Face up. Eyes widened and clear.
Wherever I go from here,
I will not go hungry.

❧ Treasure

Ax heads and sledges, musket balls and elixir bottles,
the earth cleans its room without having to be told;
as if putting tools back neatly into the case of the ground,
history knows precisely where each of us goes.

This is close to what the boy must think, he who already
has a boy buried inside him, who, like a nine-volt battery,
can be removed and handled. His head is a bottle cap,
his torso a wound mass of baling wire. And when the boy
holds this small self he can sit ringed with mushrooms
on the decaying stump of his father's childhood
and feel every turn the earth makes
driving home through the dark.

He has excavated an entire vacation. He has passed this wand
over miles of pull tabs and coffee cans teeming with grubs and beetles.
But this is his first unearthing of unadulterated sorrow,
of all he cannot remember, or forget, or undo.

He is only ten. The metal detector, which now lies
chirping across his knees, is destined for his dim closet.
But it has found him and that was worth everything.
And now that he has found himself,
these glances of light, the uncouplings
of birdsong, of leaf from leaves,
what if he were to step forward into that future,
his heart thudding like a thermos in a lunch pail,
what if he were to rise like mist from the forest floor
then turn from the flint-nicked trowel of the season?

He sees it is like those grainy silent comedies
in which someone is asked to volunteer,

then the entire cast but one steps back.
Someone has to do it. Someone has to be the past
with its drawn, saddened, weary face,
someone has to be the bullet-pocked backdrop,
that retaining wall of shame and wailing,
the collector of evidence
against which all else is measured.

❧ Pompeii

The laborers, lying down at night,
their tents layered with silt,
settled into the postures
they exhumed daily,
must have thought:

one moment we're on our way to work,
the next we're work for someone else;
one moment we're making love, the next
we've become what someone else loves to do,
brought to light by caress of chisel and hammer,
the lascivious ogling of lab techs and scholars.

But you can only guess, just as this promontory
can only look out over all that dissolves it,
the sunlight a glaze along the horizon of its going,
seabirds risen, then settling
like cinders on the water.

And so the grist of time turns out to be
not ashes, not bone shards, not even lint,
but the bread crumbs of a last meal
mostly eaten, then brushed free
to the earth.

You have tried to stay still,
God knows, you have tried
to stay pressed to the table edge,
your legs like the legs of tables,
your arms like the arms of chairs,
but here it is at last,
that destination you've been approaching
since you were a speck.

The knife on its side,
the spoon and fork arched on their backs,
the napkin crumpled, a hand
reaching over your shoulder to clear
the place setting, snuff the candle.

What is best loved betrays most acutely.
The athlete's body, the scholar's mind,
the made thing gone numb and clenched,
refusing shape.

Like beached trawlers after the storm of God,
hulls flung up and gleaming,
but split seam to seam,
here are your childhood selves
contorted in their beds,
faceup in their pasts,
that compressed soil caving
into half-open mouths,
the slender fingers of dream
plucking at their tendons.

So the sun rises, as the workers rose
again to squat over simple stoves,
to simmer and stir and sip and swallow,
in the clear dawn cold of a day
all history has come down to.

Child of tragedy from the get-go,
he was never the same
after the sacking of Troy.

He bore the blood-red logo-ed nylons
of his people. He saw
the stroller tracks converge at Delphi,

how the pillars of history
supported wrens
and the blank blue sky.

Even now he can hear the bus windows
loose in their casings, the chaotic roll
of spent camera batteries,
the rasp of that horrified chicken
in its burlap sack.

For centuries, he had traversed the remote
and each of seven wine-dark TVs,
wanting only to understand if,
and where, finally, he belonged.

At Sounion, he hunkered in the ruins
over a cold Whopper and fries,
he squatted amongst the pot shards
on the mosaic ground,

while, far in the west,
the sun gurgled down in its own blood,
and men on trawlers small as Jujubes
steered home
to slap their ancient cargo dead
against the docks.

Shot himself. Hanged himself. Shot himself.
Fell from a window just half washed.
Couldn't go. Couldn't stay. Hadn't the heart.
Stopped at a train crossing, then couldn't start.
Hit-and-run by a school bus. Lost four toes to an axe.
Hydroplaned east on a westbound road.
Took the whole vial hoping to relax.
Shot himself. Hanged himself. Starved herself.
Caught with a schoolgirl. Slipped in the tub.
Turned to God. Jumped bail. Collapsed in Jim's Pub.
Heart attack. Down's Syndrome. Cirrhosis. Stroke.
Shot himself. Hanged himself. Strung out on coke.
Incest. Seagram's. Scarred for life. Broke.
Polaroids. Videos. Chat room trysts. Tapes.
Blacked eyes. Slashed wrists. Post-marital rapes.
Curious toddlers tied with duct tape and string.
These are a few of our favorite things.

On the wax museum tour of their marriage,
every room sports its bullet-hole
or fist-sized gouge, while they,
veterans of each other,
arms around each other's waist,
recount ten years of drama,
the countless skirmishes now
phrased as casual history:

"Here's what happens when you stay out all night."

"And here's where she learned to cook breakfast first
and ask questions later."

In a day or two, something
will go chemically or financially
completely awry,
but for now, the smell of casserole
blesses the kitchen,
grandmother's hardangar and cork coasters
grace the burn-pocked coffee table.

So it is, here,
having dinner at the end of the world.
On TV, in front of the local jail,
a teen protests, her braces glinting
beneath a sign that reads
"It Was Consensuous I Swair."
Image after image,
like messages in a bottle
no one bothers to read,
like insects in a terrarium

too sluggish to feed,
like this living exhibit oblivious
to the one-way glass,
before which they snuggle,
drinking from the same long neck beer
bemoaning at leisure
how their ten-year-old
traps cats for sport,
straps them to makeshift rafts
and sends their corpses
flaming downriver.

To contain so much hatred when the hated are dead,
where does one put it? It fills the hung purses
in closets, the coat pockets, the cigar boxes,
it gleams beside the cuff links and tie clasps
in their crushed velvet spring-boxes.

If you cannot find it, it may be you
suspended in the blown glass perfume stopper,
beside the shoehorns and mortuary rulers,
the free pencils that will never be sharpened,
in the paper clips, twisted, confused, shackled
one to another.

Where, having been given the satin folds of lingerie,
their sheen and shadow like an ocean in a drawer,
do you begin?
Our parents' rooms become museums.
The hatboxes heaped with photos,

sorted by decade, mostly unlabeled,
is this where it is? The answer? The essence?
Beside the revolver under his handkerchiefs,
in our bronzed baby shoes, laced forever,
in the see-through model
of the human circulatory system,

in those branching blues and reds,
or in the broken Westclox, its alarm set for 1944?
The loose pearl she picked up, but never restrung?
The gouged surface of the Vaseline?
Where is that spark that made the world possible,

the possible world inevitable,
where is that apron that blew in furls
around your mother's waist
as she stood on the front steps to call you in?
This is as deep as you go. There is no more to them

than us. Our skins thin,
our inner lives grown cold. There is no key
taped to a drawer bottom, not one fingerprint
on one dusty light bulb, no trace of the moment
before they let go, turned their faces to the wall.

Is this what love is, this rage
to have and know? To string the pearls,
to wear that moon on a strand of her long hair,
orbiting the heart, translucent testicle,
tiny lump in the breast?
What was it that was done? Who did it

and said the others didn't need to know?
Or who did not smile and kiss you here and here,
who did not set the cocktail down to smooth your hair
with two cool hands?

How can we know,
when nothing can ever open the wall safe of silence?
And we must fashion the world again
without the painting that hung over it,
without certainty, without closure,
without them.

Red Lead, 1978

The way a boy might kick a can,
or a field goal, or a stone to skip
down one long empty street
toward a home that holds no warmth for him;
as if putting on a sock or unbuckling a belt,
some small gesture shared by all of us,
he kicked him in the face. Then,
standing like a hunter over his trophy,
one foot on the tailgate,
he dabbed blood from his boot
with a napkin.

Behind us, clouds muddied the horizon,
pigeons peered from their nests in the girders,
and the latticed shadows of the bridge
lay like a puzzle on the ground.
To the east, the broken-toothed St. Louis skyline
yawned up into haze. *It is a trial,* the stanchions said,
bound here as we are, our sorrow bestowed
so we won't float toward heaven too soon.

Spot primer, finish coat, blood, dust, and asphalt,
squabs laid gingerly down to die
by bottle caps full of water. For miles
that paper napkin rode the Missouri,
getting darker and darker, going under,
being pulled apart and into
the fierce, filthy river of everyone.

Consolidated Freight

From graveyard shift
and the loading docks of Consolidated Freight,
St. Louis was a diffuse glare,
the approaching headlights of a future
that never quite topped the worn hills and trees;

a distance that never closed—
the way the grilles of our cars gleamed
in the parking lot, till morning returned
their rusting bodies whole.
Assorted parts of an interlocking story,

all night we'd forklift marked
cartons and crates, manic decorators
bequeathed vague aesthetics and heavy furniture,
while, to the truckers gearing down our exit's curve,
we must have seemed industrious insects

swarming the lukewarm fluorescence, lost
to a task itself lost in the sum of our roles—the type
of oppressive routine that's murder, days,
but nights seems tangibly reassuring:
color-coded lines, painted on concrete

then sealed over—each free-market neuron firing
its own involuntary contribution
to the comptroller's plan—the massive overlay of routes
that was not so much map as diagram.
This was the first time my fingerprints were taken.

And I recall returning to our apprenticeship
along the demarcated zones,
working the ink from our hands, newly aware
something had been tampered with, stolen,
to deter us from stealing.

Top Pay, Home Every Weekend

Like a Kenworth diesel throttling down
the last half mile of a 6% grade,
he has snored himself from one dream
milepost to the next.
One hand on the small of his back could stop this,
but his woman's been gone
a week now Sunday and his lapdog's just happy
to sleep in the house. Don't wake him,
he's calmed by his oblivion, spooning in the mush
some truck stop waitress warms for him,
buttering the cold, ungiving toast of his future.
There is in the act of spreading oneself thin,
corner to corner, a methodical, measured intent
mere subsistence could never match. As if the life,
the time left, is no longer abstracted,
as if the moonlight diffused on his sleeping face
is of sufficient weight to keep him settled at the counter
long after the lunch rush bubbling from under the crust's edge
has cooled and congealed to a lonely few.
What, he may ask, exactly did he do to deserve this from himself?
Which pair of jeans was always bunched at his ankles,
what ambition drove him to what turnpike oasis
of dead moths and sorrow
where he idles in the mirage of this waitress's arms?

❧ Joyland

For Bret Lott

Here, between teen lovers spooning each other ice cream,
and the press of a five-putting family of four,
along the unraveling carpeted fairways
to Rapunzel, Snow White, and Sleeping Beauty,
there will be no playing through.

Soon lights will appear
in the windows of the windmill,
the tree house, the coastal beacon.
Soon the synchronized fountains will fall and rise
reminding us it has always boiled down to timing

and scorecards that tell us little
about those myths by which we've lived.
That mini-villa, is that the famed artist's colony,
snow painted on its roofs, tinsel icicles dripping from its eaves,
spiritual haven for the skittish or soon to be divorced?

Beside you and your silent wife,
on the surface of the man-made lagoon
its waters laced with blue food dye,
a real rain begins to fall, rings appearing,
as if invisible range balls were plunging from heaven.

There is, at the heart of the matter,
some wiring, a weak motor, and two sixty-watt bulbs.
Sure, the little drawbridge goes up and down
and the moat indifferently returns each ball to your instep,
but you know what's going on

behind the saloon's teensy swinging doors;
you should have been able to say no, should have

returned your watch warm to your wrist
and your keys to your hand,
and the ice bucket, unused,
to its plastic tray on the toilet tank.

And it doesn't matter whether she knows or just suspects,
you have felt the pointed tap of her putter
square on your heart saying
nothing will ever be the same.

Smoke chuffs from the teepee.
A few leaves curl at the igloo door.
You could swear you saw a field mouse in the chapel's spire.
Meanwhile, your wife is perfecting her stance,
aligning her shoulders and feet, distributing evenly

the new weight of having smelled another woman
on your clothing. Let the warning lights of the water tower
blink off and on all night, let the planes traverse the sky,
there are these holes you have dug for yourselves,
this emptiness that need be aimed at, filled.

Blind Cat at a Window

Ancient twitch of innerness,
a frequency to which
only she is attuned.
Old now, eyes scrimmed,
still she is drawn to the world's gray shadows,
the blurred motion of bird and squirrel.

Her blood, though dimmed
by canned food and tap water,
follows its course. The same
sun that spatters cool, shaded undergrowth,
warms her sill, mars her own reflection

merged with the courtyard.
There is no beyond now. Just an urge
to differentiate, perhaps, a leaf from a feather,
the feather from a butterfly drying its wings.

Though she sharpens those claws she still has,
though her unwound string snakes back
through humus, soil, and stone,
layer after layer of instinct through eons,
it is not even the chase she wants;
she couldn't digest a yearling mole.
And were we to raise the sash,
I doubt she'd go.

Parakeet

Some visits, the wire cage door was open,
others, clasped closed. Hung in the dimmest corner
of her dim front room, it still managed to glint,
the gilded grids out of place
in a Kansas farmhouse, its sprigs of plastic ivy
twined inside and out,
repositioned only for dusting.

The suspended swinging perch was always bare.
There was no bird ever spoken of,
though there must once have been.

Beatific and radiant beside the failing gas furnace,
the print of Jesus and this cage
were what warmth she knew.
And when she cooed and whistled as she cleaned,
when she trimmed fresh newspaper to line its floor,
my grandmother must have seen her own face
in the tiny mirror, felt the sloping green linoleum,
scuffed by work boots, cool against her feet.

Outside, the symmetrical rows of feed corn fields
went on without her—flocks of pigeons and crows
ascending from slackening wire
as one evanescing body.

At the Crematorium, My Son Asks Why We're All Wearing Black

These days the system is state of the art—scrims of smoke,
no odor. At least the neighbors don't protest
and the birds still gather on the tarred roof's edge
to feed on seeds pooled at drain tiles. We accumulate
and are dispersed at the traffic light out front, while within
this relay point of caskets and morgue lockers,
the husks of our fallen continue their diminishment.

We're all members of this committee, son. We serve
with our tanks full and our windows down
until in one moment
we are reduced to manila envelopes
of movie stubs, bus transfers, and address books;
in another, to pollen ruffling
the overcast, distended cloud cover of the world.

The passing lanes, the turn signals, the green and yellow lights,
the no U-turn and school crossing signs,
they all lead here.

You're old enough, now, for one dark suit and tie,
and to know exactly why
you're uncomfortable wearing it.

Til Death Do You Part: Second Ceremony

Their wavering reflection blued on a kidney-shaped pool,
the two have always been reaching for the same tray,
their emptied fluted glasses clinking in an anti-toast
to failed couplings and eclipsed engagements.
Sam's Club canapés or no, if there were ever any doubts

about their growing old, they have been put to rest.
A bee hovers around the bride's head,
the garland sweet, and then, the prolonged buzz
of an amp jacked up too high
for the reverend's lackluster recitation.

In the flowering of one revelation exists
the tight bud of another—gem-like, encrusted,
clotted with light so finely exploded
she is less bridesmaid than horizon,
a dusky pinkening from her bared collarbones up
to the infinite azure behind the sky's cumulonimbus veil.
Then, suddenly, the freshly coiffed Lhasa apso
lopes right to the groom, and with the zeal of a terrier,
sniffs his crotch.

Maybe we haven't each been to this wedding after all;
some go better than others—
no one swooning to terrazzo
or being gurneyed out to stomach pumps
while the swan ice sculpture melts east to west
along the calming surface of the well-stenciled
deep end, where, we tell ourselves,
we could all tread water if we had to.

Sky-blue tux, white cummerbund,
tie the light gray of smoke at his throat,

he has promised to honor and cherish
and have and hold
and he means well, ducking
into the limo longer than a decade of sorrow.

While here, where widows have amassed
outside the rent-a-tent, the light has texture,
we can feel it against our cuffs like untended grass,
every act taking a few tenths of a second longer,
the westernmost waning day
to sap and amber gone,
the good-byes' muted trajectories lessened
across these well-groomed, gated lawns.

Willow Run

LESSON 1:

> I've come to these rows as to a schoolroom in September,
> sliding, with my fresh pen and composition books,
> into one of few spaces not taken.
> And though it feels impolite to eat amongst the dead,
> I have crackers in my pocket, an apple, for later.
> This period, we are to cover the 18th and 19th centuries.
> The teacher's propped-up marble lectern
> is grander than his pupils', though
> his notes are yellowed pale with lichen
> and his breath is the talc of granite dust
> aloft in the air.
>
> Nothing orderly, no consistent expanse
> of well-fertilized green, no trimmed hedges
> along paved car paths back to the living.
> But there is fact, if not grandeur,
> in the oblong depressions, these sunken pits
> the exact length and width of bodies.

LESSON 2:

> There is no syllabus. You don't need indices
> to locate the past, and you can leave your irony
> at the rust-ravaged gate—through which,
> in due time, the wind conveys
> the prophylactic foils, the juice straws, the cough syrup box,
> directly to the graves of three siblings,
> ages one to three,
> whose mother lost her will to attempt a fourth.
> Like ducklings they trail her massive stone.

LESSON 3:
    What happened to those good names, Ebenezer and Silas?
    Whose sons turned their backs on the driven-upright spade
    choosing Paul and Stephen and George, to raise their hands and answer
    so that now, stiff-collared and darkly frocked,
    fenced from adjacent tennis courts,
    these side-whiskered monuments are lost even to family,
    and only tourists and lustful teens navigate
    the ditches, ruts, and speed bumps of embedded stone?

LESSON 4:
    Early in the month, a damaging storm.
    And now someone has compiled the willow and pine limbs.
    They lay entwined like legs and arms
    at the boundary line that was once a fence.
    May we all remain, the headmaster drones, heaped
    layer after layer, one on another.
    The ghosts are always in us.
    Rooted in sorrow, the willow lives.
    We can drive away,
    but we're not going anywhere.

7:30 Poems

Eastern Wyoming

Why hide where we can see you?

Because you could not find me

Why turn from fires to the inner dark?

Because the moth among sparks becomes a spark

How long can a flower be held and still be a flower?

There is no end to the ground of your hand

If the hand opens, where will the fist fall?

The fist is always a fist and grows again on your arm

How can the tree in granite flourish?

*Because its root is memory. And because one brakeman stopped
to give it water*

How can we go on this way?

There is not enough room in the world to turn your life around

Western Wyoming

Without beginning, this we know.
Eternal sequence, like the slatted snow fence
whose ends I cannot see,
the rolling slopes of rock and loam
shaped still by ocean waves of wind.

We call this a "rest area,"
but posed here like a hood ornament,
faced into the oncoming universe,
I know there's neither rest nor peace.

Here, the white line unspools behind
and love is the transaxle, the lurch forward
through static-rinsed constellations
of garbled melody and speech.

Darling, wind battered, cold to the bone,
I'm poised by the payphone
about to dial the eleven-digit code
that links your arc to mine.

East, south, west, north.
When I look out like this,
it's you I'm looking toward.

Wound

Your scar, where the kickstand gouged
or the sprocket bit as the bike went down,
that sky gleaming now after the lotion of dusk.

I touch it again with the pad of my thumb,
here, so long ago, as the ridges lie down
one with another.

Call to Prayer

I will kneel on my side of the world
looking toward you and you alone
if only you will likewise kneel.
You first.
No, me.

On Your Coast

Light and shadow are the language of clouds,
age-old evolving dialect of romance and randomness.
Infinite change. Infinite verisimilitude.
Can you hear it there, on your coast,
where our children are becoming more themselves;
the dissolution of the sea
that breaches in one slow wave over me,
calming these mountains,
damping the crow cries, one to another?

Image

The weekend carpenter on his roof a half-mile down
can be heard across the valley.
Our woodpeckers stop and turn their heads in unison.
They must think they've heard God.

Want

Kiefer, sweet boy, too far from me now,
the bobber dips so rarely in this life,
it's our job to be watching when it does.

Remember how brilliant and terrified
the little trout seemed, held up on your hook?
The gasp of joy it gave you?

Stop secreting, for a moment, what baubles you've collected
in your bedding or pillowcase,
stop and listen this once.

That stone, greened with moss,
too big to be carried home,
is called a mountain.

You can sleep with the world for a while,
but then you have to put it back.

Well of Tragedy

Beneath the weathered, ill-fitting boards,
down into the expanse,
which even through knotholes
has the depth of eons to it.

Once your eyes have filled
with that darkened, aged water,
you turn to the lustered honey of wheat fields,
changed.

From this cask, the poison
that in small doses
sets you free
of fear.

His Green Chair

Silvered watch fob, lineage of water;
acid-etched engravature of,
hairy ear and grotto of,
the world.

Palm of the ice age, cleft and riven,
I place my child hand here and here,
where the rains fall never again to know the sea
and wisps of clouds smell of rum and pipe smoke.

When will my feet, too, touch the floor?

Norway

Joints of iron, knuckles of stone,
the fjord's clouded high water marks
shift and recede.

In turn, our tide will inch back up the pilings,
the marina rustling in sleep,
stable of gentled animals,
the mountain cresting for eons
its slate like foam,
and above all, soon enough,
the visible stars.

Fathers of my father, sons of my sons,
less and less seems accident.

When the mooring chain drags along the pier,
I hear its whole length at once.

Bread Loaf, 1991

You are hungover at Dalí's house, looking at Goya prints.
The couple next to you have their arms around each other,
talking about their spouses—and grandkids—back home.
You are living in a desert with a steel plate in your head.
You are dog-paddling through the everglades in a suit of dead fish.
You are trick-or-treating disguised as a speed bump.
You are drifting toward the falls
on an inflatable mattress
during a lightning storm
while putting up an antenna.

All because the dream still glints
in the treads of your shoe,
because you cannot accept it,
because you cannot return it,
and like a dream, upon waking,
will get hurt coming true.

Pissing Off Robert Frost's Porch

For Bill Matthews

Not the side of a rowboat, granted—
no rising and falling on the wash of tides.
One drink, in honor of you, now dispersed
over daylilies and lupine as the sky Frost knew
resists its darkening, turns slate,
then charcoal gray, an operatic note
held longer than light might hope for.
What we take in, clarify, is temporary;
we pass through each other, heard again
and filtered through views
to which we're predisposed.
No ocean here, so far from home.
That death's-head moth, I know,
is neither him nor you.
The one candle that draws it forth
belongs, however briefly, to a briefer me.
And now the dogs express concern,
four or five along the valley's mile.
It will be dark until the earth has turned.
It will be dark now, for a while.

After Reading Tu Fu,

I button my shirtfront, and gathering myself,
make my script as precise as I can.
To be in the presence of great absence
requires a posture of respect.

The candle of day still feeds on his breath.
The one massing cloud, variously shaded,
draws his shroud across the mountain's face.
Once I am finished, I will follow.

But who can say when finished is.

Whittling

Deepening, one tailing at a time,
the secret is to arrive at the middle
and accept it, to have worn it down
until a whole forest fits in a suitcase,
then deeper and easier still,
tucks into the Greyhound's cargo hold,
cool, dark, skimming the pavement,
the infinitesimal wear of tire tread,
the terror of bent grasses,
paralyzed field mice, the moonlight
translucent as thin shavings of pine.

Goodbye. Goodbye. Goodbye.
Only then will the curled tufts
flower at your instep,
only then are you free
to open your hands on nothing,
to hold the stumps of your wrists to your eyes
and see.

57th Street

Skin of dream, now loosed. Let the rain
reveal its window,
that gravitational weeping toward
a cup of coffee. Whatever it takes
to be both correct and right.
Outside, the city's separate kingdoms
announce their annexations, why not
let the window reveal its tunnel of air,
why not hear the taxis calling one to another,
heads down, the plaintive wailing
of whales along elusive coasts.
Dark, deep water of want. Barge after barge
of the indifferent wounded,
faces drowning in other faces.
Scalpel's horizon, that blade explains everything,
the release in its wake opening, beyond healing,
exactly the width of a word—
bloody, light-rinsed avenue, sluice
of fire and wakefulness.

Second Skin

During your second time on earth,
you are the only thing that has changed.
No one realizes you have died
and been reset, like an heirloom gemstone.

All is as it was then.
The same wind, the same
sun-glazed boulevards.
The rinsed air still cool,
the pavement still warm and firm
beneath your feet.

Second skin, now closer to the end.
As if you and the world
shed and shed again,
yet the sameness is replaced.

There is a reason you are at the curb.

The car that sped away, the ride home,
the scent of unfolded maps you missed,
they have returned for you.

Get in.
Will you ever get a chance like this again?

THREE

Finish This

A thousand simultaneous Viking funerals,
the elm leaves drift
across my neighbor's pond.
Their trade routes mapped,
their holds full,
given over to wind
and its uncertainties.

Home is never where or what
you thought it was.

At first, the surface is everything and enough,
the glitter of vowels
on an iced cake,
mirror in which
we congratulate ourselves
dispersing and emptying and filling again.

But the undertow over which we drift
maintains its fixed course.
Beneath, in the cool silt,
at the outer reaches of light,
where the drowned offer up the gases
they've recirculated, retained, and thrived upon,
there is the namelessness
sought in all our naming.

You have felt it through the soles of your feet.
You have pulled your oar from it
like a spear from a prehistoric animal,

you have pushed off time and time again
only to find it still beneath you.

And sooner or later, you are in it for good,
your eyes open to the anonymity,
the sublime muck and motion
of the irretrievable,
of the free.

Finish This

When Gram died, her last act
was to hand back a Dixie cup
half-trembling with water
as if to say, "here, finish this."
My mother took it, separating the fingers,
thin and glossy with illness,
then guiding the whole arm down
to its place across her chest.
I was on the other side,
the hospital bed rail
pushing one cool shirt button into me
as if I were a doorbell. "I'm out here,"
Death was saying, "You don't have a lot of time,
you coming or not?"
The railing gave a little, sideways,
and since there was nothing left
but those most accidental of sounds—
the involuntary frictions of left/right,
up/down, in/out,
the sound of loose tire chains
in the back of a pickup,
of two emaciated swords
meeting farther and farther away—
that final letting go of the guard
by which all week she had pulled herself up toward me,
was a release into silence, a recognition
of the true completeness of every gesture.
And having relayed to me that dry, barely tangible kiss,
she could stop now, thereby seeming calmly to recede.
Outside, the cold white ashes of eons
piled high against the curbs

and Death leaned on his shovel
near a narrow, heavily salted path into underground parking,
and the car stalled,
and it seemed for a moment,
the past so completely with me, so heavy and sodden,
I'd never turn the key again.
That was when I remembered the Dixie cup,
the pale purple lilacs ringing its lip,
and how my mother raised it like a shot glass to her own mouth
then chose merely to sip.

❧ Dark Black

Indelible, less color
than psychic stain,
something so ancient and pervasive
it has become the norm
there at the tightened corners
of great-great-grandmother's mouth,
the browning daguerreotype photo
behind smudged glass.
At what level is clarity struck?
In which generation do the masks become faces,
do the men and women put aside
their spectacles on bed stands
and see, not themselves,
but each other
in themselves?

Last night, an hour after I turned off her lights,
I heard my daughter sobbing.
Her goldfish was dead,
the story's stepmother was mean,
some boy had pushed her down at school.
There was no rest there, in the dim light cast
by her porcelain lamb—
she could not let herself sleep.

How does it first enter us?
Wading the river? Walking the wet, blackened shore?

"Dark black," she says, when asking
her brother to hand her a crayon,
the deepest one, the one
that is like looking down a well

far past sadness and decay
into the lustrous reservoir of carbons and clay.

For as long as she lives,
she will be that wick,
burning, blackening, drawing
upon the deep oils of beginnings and ends,
that which she knows but does not know she knows.

Even two decades out of context, I'd have known
the handwriting—the crimped, fastidious, formal
embodiment of her severity;
which is to say, the imposition of her will,
which is to say, her puritanical need
to be indelibly of use.

"This bucket has a hole in it,"
it reads, in permanent marker,
the pail itself, brittle now,
and lined with another, smaller, pail,
handleless and nestled precisely within,
its own intact bottom home
to nineteen and one-half clothespins.

Twenty years since her death,
I have opened the cabinet
of what is still her kitchen.
The laundry soap is fresh,
the roach baits new,
but this bucket is what she chose to bequeath,
just as this trailer, now our summer place,
was to her all the future we'd ever need.

Sometimes, on clear nights,
the moon-silvered clotheslines
seem webbed and endless in these lots;
hopelessly interlaced, hopelessly finite,
hopelessly unable to retain what form
mortal clothing can ever offer.

As when a two-year-old cups her palms
to the hand lantern her brother holds in his,

sometimes what we want
can be glimpsed, trembling
in the surface of our coffee,
sometimes we fully sense
how life's not ours.

Off/on, open/closed, empty/full:
my daughter is learning the absolutes
she'll spend the rest of her life
struggling to transcend.

She sits up like a big girl. She tips
the bucket between her legs on the floor.
She takes all she can from it
and reaches—what else?—for more.

After the Sea Parts, My Daughter Walks among Gravestones

Don't be fooled. Though the ocean would give anything to lie down,
a dry towel on its forehead, fully relaxed, across the whole earth,
the sea floor is just another shore.

And what a slathering that sea makes of it: the weeds, the driftwoods,
all the night's dead washed back and forth. Imagine the pressure
of that sky in your ears, that deep a blue in you, that useless plea
to all the pleasure craft bobbing above the drowned.

This deep, we can barely hear the motors' throbbing, the keen
of riggings and keels along shallow reefs. This deep,
the intensity of last things puts its shine on the coffin handles,
the sunlight of the fifties casts storm doors in bronze,
and the warped antennae are twisted till all pales with the news.

You could say the dead keep choosing for us and choosing wrong—
you'd be right. Tide pools of genealogy to be sloshed through and
    around.
No ship tacks back. And though the lapdog swims in circles on the
    mealy lawn,
though porcelain dolphins arc eternal from their pedestals on sills,
your grandmom's 12-quart kettle can't now soothe her swollen feet.

Fatherhood

Your life will be half-over when you arrive
at this porch yourself, the stars close and clear
through your breath, the moist, misted breath
of the one world we all contribute to, fully present,
quivering with distances. And if the backlight
from your kitchen door throws a skewed rectangle
into which you fit like a coffin,
know that I'm behind you then, helping you
not to turn around, helping you to stand straight up,
taking in the blades of cold, going on and on,
though your body stays rooted firmly
at the edge of all you've built.

Once my dirt is turned, your gardening begins,
and so I offer this soil I didn't know I was making,
this darkness from which flower light arcs,
perennial, inextinguishable,
spearing all with beauty.

Drive the trowel deep, separate the ribs,
tamp far into me your guilt and shame. I will
no longer be separate from you then, together
as we could not be while I lived. We'll be as lilies
sprouted from the same bed, having gouged out our place,
now bowed with rain, now upturned and listening.

And I will be with you on your father's rounds,
this late, when the only sound is your neighbor's heat pump,
and the hanging plants twisting on their chains,
once you have been compelled back into the house,
floorboards shifting beneath the carpet.

The nightlight in the children's bathroom
glows on the bath toys in the hall.
Nothing has been put back,
which means all is where it ought to be, and
the children, breathing arduously after a long day
of touching everything they own at least twice,
seem to have fallen from jungle gyms
into their beds, their lips dry when you kiss them,
their faces cool, their hearts rhythmic in some dream place.

From one room to another in the house of yourself,
surprising a silverfish, straightening frames,
repositioning your mother's pillows on the olive couch;
that's how I see you, turned inward, finally,
having acquired something to lose,
a shadow in boxer shorts bending over the sleepers
with the weight of fatherhood
like a sleeping newborn on your chest,
her ear to your heart.

Soon you will turn even deeper into the house
and the warmth of a woman who will forgive your absence
if only you turn fully and to her alone.

Just a little while longer, you'll think,
then I'll go to bed,
just one more moment
and perhaps they'll smell your skin, sense you there
perhaps dream of you watching over them,
doing what you can to see the darkness for what it is
to leave it outside pressed against the windows,
leaning in its turn, over all of you.

❧ Sill

On the kitchen sill,
in the square brick house
my aunt aged and died in,
the flawless hand-blown pear
will neither rot nor last.

My daughter, too young
to ever think of this again,
once took it down
and placed it in a bowl,
with the breakfast oranges.
She'd thought it lonely, I guess,
with just the sunlight against it,
that single breath,
exhaled, perhaps, just after lunch,
smelling of cheese and peach schnapps.

Dust is the pollen of our dying,
even children sense this,
and after she'd wiped it clean
with her flowered dress,
she held it suspended
by its delicate, disproportionate stem
and lowered it into the wooden bowl.

Her great-aunt, though,
had little patience with disorder,
couldn't bear the clean, unblemished outline
where it had originally been,
and that was that.

Moments ago, after assurance that her family
would all recognize each other in heaven,
my daughter asked who would take care of her things.
And when I said her babies could, she cautioned
that babies can't even take care of themselves.

Neither can we, of course, never tall enough
to reach the light switch ourselves,
never able to drink from the wall-mounted fountain of awareness,
we stuff our pockets with beads and bottle-caps,
we organize our knick-knacks as best we can.

My aunt's squat, miniature tract house was razed.
Her windowsill exists only in the heaven of children.
The pear, it could be anywhere,
like the last breath of the old German who made it.
Likewise, her porcelain salters
and the hummingbird hovering
at its glass flower.

The Lion's Share

They are gathered as if to be told a story.
Three kids, perhaps seventeen, facing
the headstone, a pastel bedsheet beneath them.
That bottle of wine on its side in the grass?
Safe to assume it is empty, safe to assume
the center girl being comforted, leaning
forward as if speaking, drank the lion's share;
her hair now mussed, her posture so clearly
deflated and spent. The other girl and boy,
they are here because they promised to be.
One year to the day, perhaps, since the death
they have in common. A toast, an awkward
eulogy, a token gift, all of it more difficult
than they'd bargained for.

And you and I, reader, we are parked in the cemetery, why?
Because I thought it a shortcut to a parallel road?
Because I needed to feel for a moment the fact of my own life?
A sparse flock of starlings is feeding in the short grass.
The wind flutters in memorial flowers, even the artificial ones.
Whatever the reason, I am grateful you've come.
So much that needs saying. In such little time.

Natural Causes

Because my son saw the round hay bales—
1200 pounds apiece, shrink-wrapped in white plastic—
lining the fields,
we have had to search all evening
for marshmallows.
Two stores were out. Another
had one stale and shrunken bag.
The fourth had three bags, but no wood for fire,
so we went back to the first.
And I needed newspaper to start the kindling,
which is how I know Earl Softy died Monday,
at home, in his sleep, of natural causes. So rarely
we know how we know what we know.
Don't turn the page. Sit with us awhile,
here by the fire in New Hampshire.
Have a marshmallow.
Because my wife and I love each other
and wanted something of, and more than, ourselves;
because my little son has imagined heaven in the pasture land,
even death tastes sweet.

Pleasing. That simple
a word. Like a child and his dog drinking

from the same hose, one horse nuzzling another,
two birds sitting so close they seem
to have only two wings.

It's because I'm going to see you
I see these things.

Yesterday, I thought that dusk
was a kind of rain. Darkness fell and kept falling
until I believed it was something solid.

Now I see that when the blind remove their dark glasses,
when they put them on the bed stand before sleep,
there is a difference that they know.

This is when you smile the mysterious half-smile
of those in love. Like miles of stone fence
on a moonlit pillow.

All of this because my eyes are already looking for you.
Because of you I can put my arm out the window

without fear. Because of you no tears
well in the spoons of these houses,
no one flinches

and the bodies of husbands and wives
are like warm bread to each other.

They believe that the moon

will touch the earth lightly on its waist
and that the earth will turn.

I'm really going to see you, I know
because I really believe these things.
And because I believe them,

the cat slouching under that small tree
where the two wrens sat was driven away,
was beaten.

I know this now.
My skin feels pleasant suddenly
as the darkness veers around it.

And the dog sleeps lightly at the child's door.
And night is falling short of the ground.

The commas are the first to go,
well before periods, those
deeply drill-pressed holes denoting
what we know as last.
The dead don't need punctuation,
blended as they are
in equilibrium beyond syntax,
their final wishes and scripture
thinning on the thinning stone.

Solon's tuberculosis, Elizabeth's grief
at having outlived four fated children,
relieved now by the laying on of weather's hands.
For the body, it is as when the wedges of split wood
have burned long and deeply, softening enough
to collapse in halves and thirds onto the grate.
But the burning of stones is interminable and even,
the sun, day by day, fading the vinyl
of mobile homes beside the graveyard,
oblong mausoleums lit nightly
with the blue wash of TV.

Sometimes I stop at the spigots,
fill the watering can caretakers provide,
and douse the driest, neglected flowers—
sometimes I just drive past.
Or sometimes, my car's aerodynamics
a bit too coffin-like,
I just walk from grave to grave,
sensing the give of the earth,
the vaults' contours, the waterlines'
crisscross grid above the bones.

If there's anything left to be said,
I don't know what it is.
I just repeat what the stones say.
And the wind, as you've guessed already,
will have the last word, anyway.

snowfall within   the turned dirt blessed
only spade phrasings cadences   only
a left vest pocket in which the silvered sun sets

                                        always
a chilled equilibrium   always molecular and whole
the sequenced spray of wrens

                        bouquet
for the dead   right to left
the field's waves break   and the epilogue gets read

closer to infinity than 1922   having trudged
dune   after mercurial dune
to this kitchen table   this soup kettle
boiled down to saucepan   the potpourri
of two husbands and five children   the peeling
Audubon wallpaper,   winged, lifting off

ave ave   raise the postman's last red flag
let the scrolled fleur-de-lis storm door
shudder once   and rest ajar

surrender to snow the risen water

After Rain

Sometimes, night quieted,
what's real soaks in further;
the mesh screens gemmed by halogen,
my neighbors' doorbell switch
like a moon within reach,
the lilies nodding on their stems
like exhausted horsemen.
Denied the old illusion of ownership,
I have opened somehow,
but for once, nothing is leaving or lessened.

The journey is long.
The journey is not long.
Moths drink their fill at the screens,
the caught rain glistening.
What conscious moment
is not, in essence, worship;
what state more vulnerable
than the attentive mind upturned?

We bear forth our sparks from psychic fire,
each family a series of contained blazes,
each patio torch a signal pyre,
our longing eternal,
and though the skin thins,
our inner lives grow cold,
there is, always, this black frock
nightfall offers—
the comfort, finally,
of tenderness and humility and weakness,
the calm after rain
and before the slate's clearing.

Snow. A nit's weight
on the hair of our necks,
the blessed host of the past,
right there, just so.

Turn into it, this once.
It's time to become the lake surface,
time to claim your face.

Soon the present
will cool enough to touch,
you can lay you down
in the outline you once were,

smoke still adrift
from the original fire.
Cup the moth's spark
in your hands.
Open your mouth and take
the dissolution
on your tongue.

No one else remembers
all that you remember.
If you don't carry it,
who will?

⟿ Acknowledgments

The author wishes to thank the editors of the following magazines in which these poems first appeared:

Black Ridge Review ("Better Homes and Gardens," "Blind Cat at a Window," "Willow Run"); *Cider Press Review* ("The Museum at the End of the World"); *Crazyhorse* ("After Rain," "Fatherhood," "The Lion's Share"); *Greensboro Review* ("Eastern Wyoming," "This Bucket Has a Hole in It," "Til Death Do Us Part: Second Ceremony"); *Green Mountains Review* ("At the Crematorium, My Son Asks Why We're All Wearing Black"); *Indiana Review* ("Pompeii"); *Mid-American Review* ("Red Lead, 1978"); *Poetry Miscellany* ("57th Street," "Odyssey"); *SLATE Magazine*/www.slate. com ("Finish This"); *Smartish Pace* ("After Reading Tu Fu," "Call to Prayer," "Dark Black," "His Green Chair," "Image," "Norway," "On Your Coast," "Second Skin," "Treasure," "Want," "Well of Tragedy," "Western Wyoming," "The White Doves of Topeka," "Whittling," "Wound"); *Solo* ("Pissing Off Robert Frost's Porch"); *Tar River Poetry* ("Inner Rooms," "Pail of Eggs," "Rest Darling Sister Rest").

"After the Sea Parts, My Daughter Walks Among Gravestones," "Red Lead, 1978," and "Joyland," appeared in *Poets of the New Century* (David R. Godine, 2001).

"On the Way to See You," first appeared in *Barbells of the Gods* (Ampersand Press, 1988).

My eternal gratitude to The Frost Place of Franconia, New Hampshire for a residency at which many of these poems began. Tony Hoagland, and David Rivard—thanks, as always.

Mark Cox is the author of *Barbells of the Gods* (1988), *Smoulder* (1990), and *Thirty-Seven Years from the Stone* (1998). His honors include a Whiting Writers' Award, a Pushcart Prize, the Oklahoma Book Award, the Society of Midland Authors Poetry Prize, and a Burlington-Northern Faculty Achievement Award. He served as the twenty-fourth Poet-in-Residence at The Frost Place, and has received fellowships from the Kansas Arts Commission, the Vermont Council on the Arts, and the Bread Loaf Writers' Conference. The chair of the Department of Creative Writing at the University of North Carolina–Wilmington, he lives in Wilmington with his wife, Karin, and their three children.